I'd Rather Be President

A HANDBOOK FOR EXPECTANT CANDIDATES, BY

CHARLES ELLIS AND FRANK WEIR

ILLUSTRATED BY WALT KELLY

SIMON AND SCHUSTER, NEW YORK

CONTENTS

1

Who, Me?

"My proposition is not exactly absurd."
—GEORGE F. WILLIAMS, Massachusetts *

I N THIS year of crisis the American public, the oldest and wealthiest employer of Presidents in the world, is voicing a familiar complaint: too few men of promise seem willing to explore the possibilities of employment in this field. All too frequently the sign PRESIDENT WANTED attracts but a single outstanding applicant from the millions of eligibles of one major party—sometimes both. Yet today, more than ever before, few careers offer such tempting rewards to the American of industry and patriotism, with an itch to impress his neighbors, as that of running for President or other high office.

* This and succeeding quotations at chapter headings are taken from the proceedings of the Republican and Democratic National Conventions, 1892–1908.

The man who runs for President is assured tremendous prestige. People will laugh at his lamest jokes. His name, for a time, becomes imbedded in the language, a signal for rejoicing or sulphurous debate. He travels to remote counties of the Union, first-class, expenses paid. His mannerisms, accent and boyhood pranks freshen neighborhood gossip. Everyone has a chance to win and become President of the United States. Even the also-rans are privileged to participate in a hallowed national ritual.

Why, then, should men who might make significant contributions to the profession of Running for High Office spurn its exhilarating challenge? Surveys indicate that the scarcity of applicants stems not from any lack of interest but from the average man's conviction that he does not know how to run and cannot learn.

How often has a chance suggestion—a newspaper headline or a passing remark of your wife ("A fine President *you'd* make!")—set you to dreaming of a White House career?

Diplomatic receptions in the East Room, forty winks on the Lincoln bed, congenial week ends with secret-service agents at a sylvan retreat, your own private plane . . .

And then you puncture the bubble with a hopeless "I wouldn't know where to begin."

Fortunately, this need not be true. A campaign for President is not a mystery beyond the capabilities of the uninitiate. It is a connected series of operations conducted according to well-established traditions, customs and usages—what might be called campaign etiquette—by which any candidate may chart his course from the first glimmer of ambition right down to election day.

Campaign etiquette is nothing more than the rules which politicians have mutually agreed upon to make public life essentially simple and gracious. There is nothing vague or "hard to understand" about them. They are, above all, intensely practical, tested by a long process of trial and error. The hard-boiled politician observes these rules because they *work*.

How much wiser it is to learn and apply the lessons of experience than to suffer embarrassment and possible failure! As you become expert in their use, you will find yourself playing the game with greater facility, to your added enjoyment and profit.

Doubtless you yourself, given the time—and the money—could hit upon the proper conduct for each of the many situations you would encounter in the course of a routine campaign. But without the wisdom of the past to guide you—especially in today's complex, swiftly moving civilization—you might find yourself baffled by an unfamiliar problem. As a novice, ignorant of the rules, you risk a misstep, loss of confidence and—what is worse—votes.

These rules, though precise and well known to the politician of experience, until now have been set down only in scattered, inaccessible records. This volume is an attempt to codify them and restate them in simple terms so that they may be mastered at the cost of but a few minutes of your time each day, less time than you now spend on the evening paper. If it persuades you to run for President, it will have served its purpose.

2

Yes, You

"*. . . without thought of office or preferment.*"
—WINFIELD SCOTT HAMMOND, Minnesota

WE WILL assume, then, that you'd like to be President. There is no need to feel ashamed and unworthy as you make the confession. It's always possible you might make a good one. Besides, you are a citizen and a taxpayer and you can hope as well as the next man.

16

The hoping stage is as far as the average candidate ever gets. For—we may as well be frank—the opening maneuvers of a Presidential campaign are the most delicate in the entire field of politics, demanding the iron will of a Bismarck, the subtlety of an Iago and the coyness of a Minnie Mouse.

The first rule is inviolable. It is this: the candidate must not admit that he is one. The role of the candidate, in other words, is that of the maiden in courtship. Watch a maiden "surrender" to a suitor and you will understand the phrase "the office seeks the man." Incidentally, if women are ever taken seriously as Presidential possibilities, men, the jig is up.

One test of your aptitude for this line of work will be in the way you exploit your background. By the time you've decided to run there's little you can do about your past. The idea is to put your background to work for you. Let's suppose you are the businessman type. Then boast that you "know nothing about politics." You know what it is to "meet a payroll." You believe in more business in government and less government in business. If there has never been a strike at your plant, fine. It shows you get along with the working man. Or there has been a strike, a long and bad-tempered one. All right, you believe in the give and take of collective bargaining.

Maybe you've been feeding at the public tr—— (holding public office, that is) since you could shave. You have in that case "devoted years to the science of government," years that brought you into intimate contact with the problems of business—especially small business.

If yours has been the profession of arms, your experience has taught you that the military should always be subordinate to civilian authority. And who, better than you, can appreciate what war really means?

The point is that, whatever your background, the complexities of modern life and the critical problems that will face our nation during the next four years cry aloud for the type of leadership that can be provided only, by the most amazing coincidence, by you. You will be tempted to join the cry. Don't. This is where your "friends" take over.

"But," you may say, "my friends don't want me to be President—not the ones who really know me." You have fallen into a common error. A "friend" in the political sense need not be an intimate companion or even a close acquaintance. He may find you obnoxious, irritating or dull. Nobody bets on a horse because he loves the jockey. Once you are elected President you will have lots of friends. Those who got in on the ground floor will be friendliest of all.

Some of your friends, in the nature of things, will be professional politicians. They can be invaluable, but keep them in the background. The first man to be struck with the conviction that you are Presidential timber should be a political nitwit, at least so far as the public knows. He describes himself as a "dirt farmer," a "country lawyer" or a "plain businessman" who is gravely concerned for the welfare of the country. This country, he announces (gravely), needs a man who can guide it through the troubled times that lie ahead. You—it's startling how these things work out—you are that man. Thus you have taken the first hurdle. You have been "mentioned" as a candidate.

Nothing is impossible and you may even have a handful of friends who'd like to see you in the White House because they are genuinely fond of you and think you'd make a first-rate President. The notion may not have occurred to you, but it did to Shakespeare. "Grapple them to thy soul with hoops of steel." Their enthusiasm might be infectious.

Your function at this point is to provide the theme for the Presidential overtures, the hot air for the trial balloons. Make a simple appeal the voter can understand—or thinks he can. You balanced the budget in your state, for example; luckily in some states unbalanced budgets are against the law. Or you sent a racketeer to jail; you're the gangbuster type. Possibly you shouldered your way to stardom at a televised committee hearing. Political reputations have been built on less. So long as you are under 50 you may offer yourself as the "young liberal" of your party. Whichever role you choose, experience indicates that you are a "middle-of-the-road thinker." This follows Lincoln's Law: You can fool all of the people some of the time. The middle of the road appears on no map, but it is the super highway of politics.

3
Well, Maybe

"I am complimented and flattered by your invitation."
    —James K. Campbell, Ohio

HAVING ARRANGED to be mentioned for President, you will be asked to comment on this development. Here, too, your course has been charted carefully by precedent. It starts with an expression of profound disbelief and dissolves into a modest disclaimer, to show that you harbor no unworthy personal ambition. It proceeds to the hearty laugh—proof that you can appreciate a joke on yourself—and thence to a few murmured words of humble gratitude for the compliment.

Your normally candid nature may rebel at all this pussyfooting. You'd make a darned good President, you think, so why not come right out and say so? Remember, you have others to think of. Millions are depending on you to preserve tradition.

So long as the country can produce candidates who won't be rushed into admitting they *are* candidates, people and politicians will have something to cling to. Don't deprive them of it.

Indeed, keep your friends plugging away along the You-for-President line. Remark publicly, with a "twinkle" in your eye, that it's good publicity for your state. Soon you will be ready for the next move, a formal announcement that you have "authorized no one to speak" for you or to conduct a campaign for you and, while you are "flattered by all this talk," you have not the slightest intention of running for anything.

If you mean it, nothing is easier than to drop out of the race, and this book is not meant for you. Scholarly commentators will soberly remind the public that William Tecumseh Sherman had a way of making himself clear on this point: "If nominated I will not run; if elected I will not serve."

Don't stoop to answer this yourself, but have a "friend" point out indignantly that "of course" no American can refuse to serve his country, regardless of the sacrifice it entails. The troublemakers will cackle that you needn't sacrifice for *them*. Obviously a case of sour grapes. Pay no attention.

It's time you were making a public appearance. Prevail
upon some organization to offer you its annual award for
"outstanding service." The award need not be expensive (a
scroll will do) and the citation need not tell in exactly what
respects your service stood out. Plenty of organizations will
be glad to make such a presentation. They will get publicity;
what is more to the point, so will you. The real purpose of
the award is to give you the opportunity to make a speech,
the first of your campaign.

On this occasion, if you are an accomplished talker, pour
it on. If you are tongue-tied, with an abrasive monotone and
awkward gestures, have your friends prime the audience in
advance. You, they explain with pride, despise the show-
man's tricks that glib-tongued glamour boys use to mask
their insincerity. You simply talk, man to man, straight from
the shoulder, about what's on your mind.

As a matter of fact, you tell your audience, you're not going to make a speech at all. You're simply going to "think out loud" on some of the problems of the day. But you are going to be specific. Denounce lack of preparedness, oppressive taxes, corruption in high office, big-business domination (if you're not *in* big business), the stirring up of class against class, impractical idealists and cynical materialists and the Japanese beetle.

Conclude with the sober reflection that if these problems are not faced squarely by a vigorous, imaginative and courageous leadership, you fear for the future of our country. (Leave yourself out of it; you are still not seeking office, remember?) The troublemaker may snort that your deep concern is a suspiciously recent development. Scorn him. He is trying to buck the inexorable tide of a well-planned campaign and he knows it.

This speech probably will touch off requests for your co-operation in a television visit to your home. If it doesn't, a word to a friend at one of the networks might swing it. Get rid of any ideas you may have about keeping your domestic arrangements out of this operation. You can't just take it for granted that people will assume you have a home life; you have to prove, to everybody's astonishment, that you have a home and live in it.

When the TV cameramen "drop in" they can find you doing almost anything so long as it isn't lying back in a contour chair with your mouth open. That would create an undesirable impression of indolence. Be surprised running a power mower, or boning up on world affairs in your study. A room can be arranged for the purpose, complete with books.

If your children are of the right age, and can be bribed to behave themselves, have them dash in demanding a "ride on Daddy's back." It's risky, but sure-fire if you can bring it off. In case you're a grandfather, a little snuggling on your knee is about all you'll be up to. Before you say a few words to the mike, blandly feigning inability to understand why anybody should be interested in you, have your wife point out your "favorite" chair.

A word about that favorite chair. Most people who have lived long enough to qualify for elective office have acquired along the way a series of preferences about unimportant things, and nobody thinks anything of it. But in a candidate it is regarded as a comforting sign of steadiness of character. As the campaign goes on, have your friends drop references to your "favorite" pipe, your "favorite" dog, fishing rod, hat and so on. They needn't mention your favorite blonde.

So much for the home front. In these days it is sound practice to take a trip abroad to "study world conditions at first-hand." Your friends may tip off the papers that you're going, and then it is all right for you to confirm the story. Admit that you have been "concerned for some time now about the way things are going." If you are a member of Congress or an official of the administration in power, the taxpayer will pick up the check for the junket. Otherwise you go "just as a private citizen." Either way, the rules of the game prevent the administration from stopping you. It will be following the elementary tactic of pretending it never heard of you.

Leaders in foreign capitals will greet you effusively. This may surprise you, but stop and think a moment. For all they know, you may soon be President, and they did not attain leadership by snubbing the man with the money. You will also find that you can confer with the military brass of this country at foreign bases. Praise the commanders for doing a "magnificent job under tremendous handicaps." Don't neglect the enlisted men—there are more of them. Giving a

private a lift in your plane is always effective if photographers are around to record the magnanimous deed.

Your trip will have convinced you that American prestige abroad is endangered either by "bungling and lack of policy" or because the tactics of the opposition have led the world to feel that "America is divided." Say anything except what you think ought to be done about it. That is not your job—yet.

Hint ominously that the country would be stunned if you could reveal half of what you learned on the trip. If you work in Washington, by the way, observe that it's an advantage to be in the center of things and you're glad to be back. If you are located elsewhere, be thankful you're not in "that madhouse" but instead are close to the grass roots where you can preserve a sense of proportion.

Your office staff, if it has been doing its job, will have a shock in store for you—two shocks in fact—and you must lose no time in reporting them to the public. During your absence, you disclose, a veritable tidal wave of mail has come to your office from persons interested in your candidacy—"particularly our younger voters." In a way, you confess, this is more than a little embarrassing since you have never, in your wildest imagination, thought of yourself as a White House possibility. A thing like this, you add, makes a man feel "humble, very humble."

The other shock is this: Without consulting you, your friends have been quietly "sounding sentiment" in various parts of the country. The results of this survey, as they tell it to you, have been truly amazing. The demand that you announce your candidacy amounts to nothing less than a "tremendous surge" from voters in all walks of life. How, your friends will ask themselves, can you hesitate any longer?

The survey technique is foolproof. It requires practically no work at all because there is no way, short of a Presidential election itself, to check its accuracy. The chance is remote, but suppose some unsportsmanlike chap (who is promoting his own man) does demand facts and figures. The attack may be parried deftly by one of your friends.

This survey, he will bark indignantly, was conducted in strictest confidence. And he will not be tricked into betraying that confidence, not even to gain political advantage. That will take care of nosey questions from the opposition, but news reporters are something else again. Sooner or later one of them will want to know: "Are you a candidate for President or not?"

He will want a direct answer, but don't let him have it. There are several ways out. One is: "I do not seek public office; I do not shun public responsibility."

Another: "No one should volunteer for this mighty work; none should shirk it if drafted."

A third: "I'm not running for anything; I'm not running away from anything."

Or the reliable: "The office should seek the man, not the man the office."

4

Duty's Clarion Call

"So far we have not made any mistake."
—Joseph B. Foraker, Ohio

IN A WAY, to come out flatly and admit that you are running for President takes half the fun out of the game. By this time you've probably learned to appreciate the subtle pleasure of approaching definite statements without actually saying anything. It's an enjoyable exercise of your skill and wit. But you cannot linger at this stage, much as you enjoy it. Sooner or later you have to pass on to the next.

Here again the rules are flexible. Technically, it is possible for a candidate to wait coyly in the wings until, flushing prettily, he is pushed on stage to accept the nomination. This approach is risky, though, and calls for the rugged constitution of a fullback and the emotional make-up of a flounder.

At the other extreme is the candidate who really has no choice in the matter. If this is your second or third outing in the Presidential stakes, everyone knows what you're up to. You may spend a few weeks of well-publicized indecision, just to stay within the rules. Then, since you are not fooling anyone anyway, come right out and say it: "I want to be President." Imply that other hopefuls who are still digging their toes in the carpet are being less than candid with the public. Imply, too, that the public resents this dilly-dallying. On being told this, a part of the public *will* begin to resent it.

Possibly, for reasons of your own, you will choose neither extreme but a compromise of the two. Explain that, because of your unique talents and devotion to duty, you have been entrusted with a job that forbids you to "play politics." Nothing, you declare (solemnly), can influence your iron resolve in this matter except an unmistakable call to higher service.

That call may come at any convenient time, and you're the only one who has to hear it. Then a forthright statement of your candidacy is in order.

For this momentous announcement, on or off the air, your manner must be solemn and humble, somewhat wistful, a bit sad, with the dedicated fervor of a crusader. You have, you say, pondered this question long and prayerfully. You have sought the advice of your friends and, of course (with a tender glance at her), your wife. What comes first—your own personal inclinations or the country's welfare? There can be, you have concluded reluctantly, but one answer. No man could refuse a call to duty. You are in this fight to the finish.

35

Bear down on abstract nouns. Demand justice, honor, thrift, generosity, tolerance, courage and decency in public affairs. This in itself advances your campaign a long step. At one stroke you have indicted every last opponent as an unfair, biased, pusillanimous, stingy ne'er-do-well of questionable habits and, at the same time, you have upheld the highest traditions of politics.

The newcomer, having thus openly confessed his yearning for office, will for a time feel like a man who has wandered into the lobby of the Waldorf-Astoria in his shorts. You may react this way, and, if you do, it does you credit. The feeling will soon wear off. For good or ill you are on the treadmill and there is no stopping. The next move will be an interview or press conference with you as a new candidate. Within limits, this is subject to your control.

The place may be your home or your office, depending on several factors. If your principal opponent is the fearless prosecutor or busy executive type, your home is the best bet. The setting should not be too luxurious, however, and if your home runs to ankle-deep rugs, built-in bars and a modern décor, shift the scene to the office. Don't forget, the TV cameras will be watching. Either way, the theme of your first post-announcement offering should be amazement, gratification and—we hate to harp on this—humility. For every candidate who has been defeated because of his principles, a dozen have ruined themselves by their own cockiness.

Start by expressing your intense gratefulness for the public reaction. Point to a stack of telegrams—old ones will do—that have been coming in all morning. Confess wryly that you've been able to do no more than sample them. The realization that so many people, especially young people, or

women, or veterans, or wage earners, see eye to eye with you on the grave issues that confront us all has been heart-warming indeed, you say. After you get the hang of it you'll be able to toss of remarks like these without conscious effort or shame.

Here is the opportunity to give the public another peek into your private life. If all this takes place in your office, turn the job over to your secretary—not a luscious young dish but a crotchety old harridan whose one redeeming feature is a savage loyalty to you. Her flinty eye can soften at the mention of your name; this will be noted in your favor.

At home, the same assignment goes to your wife. She can disclose, in answer to a planted question, that of course you slept like a baby after your big speech the night before, that you got up at precisely 6:15 as usual, walked the dog or performed some other homely duty, and ate a hearty breakfast of eggs—"sunny side up."

Now that the cat is out of the bag you can move about and speak more freely—but still cautiously. Here the public's healthy curiosity can be turned to good advantage. Some persons find Presidential candidates only slightly less fascinating than giveaway winners, beauty-pageant contestants and professional comedians. As a live, accredited candidate you will be able to attract sizable audiences either in person or on television.

At this stage you won't get many offers of free air time just to make speeches. More likely you'll be asked to appear on a panel show, or perhaps a quiz show with you being quizzed. If you're a little slow on the answers, better avoid these. Interviews on radio or television also have their hazards. Don't let yourself be mousetrapped by a squad of commentators whose stock in trade is a knack for embarrassing public figures. And steer clear of teen-age interviewers; they'll toss in nasty questions just to show off. Television producers anxious to cash in on your modest (at this point) fame will ask you to take part in shows involving getting smeared with chocolate sauce and whipped cream. It's up to you to decide right now whether you think the voters want their candidate for President to look like a piece of French pastry.

Speaking invitations call for careful screening. A chamber of commerce, for example, is likely to be interested in your stand on taxes. A labor union might want your views on jobs and wages. You can avoid these pitfalls by appearing at nonpartisan affairs, at round-table discussions, or as a guest star. A home-town high-school gathering makes an ideal audience for your purpose. The idea is not new, but nothing has been found to beat it.

The pupils themselves can be disposed of with standard references to the American way of life, hardy pioneers and the challenge of the future. Tell their parents you are delighted at the opportunity to meet with them again. You and they think alike, you remark comfortably, keeping out of trouble. But now that you are a candidate you think they may want to "look you over." That is how you would feel if your positions were reversed, and you think they should have the chance to see the "cut of your jib."

This creates an air of frankness about you that is most

desirable. The appearance of frankness, in fact, should be featured throughout your campaign. Note: the *appearance* of frankness. Genuine frankness is likely to backfire. It makes some people vaguely uneasy and resentful.

It is a good idea at this point to arrange two or three speeches in quick succession in some state or section of the country. This—you may count on it—will be called a "whirlwind speaking tour." It has merits that should be obvious to you by this time. You get credit for taking as little time as possible away from your job, whatever it is. You make the politicians backing your opponents wonder what kind of slick deal you are rigging in *that* state.

In connection with your travels, there's a little trick that never fails, and you might as well learn it now. Let's say you're from Ohio. Here and there in other states unimpressive characters will be shoved forward, or will shove themselves forward, and announce that they too are from Ohio.

"*You're* from *Ohio!*" you exclaim, beaming. That's all there is to it. Your manner says that this is the most miraculous, most heart-warming thing imaginable. That you should meet someone from Ohio in, say, Indiana is more than you dared hope for. In this way you take a big step toward passing the loyalty-to-his-state test that every candidate is subjected to.

When the opportunity presents itself, as it is bound to eventually, pounce on some act, statement or policy of the opposition party. Denounce it indignantly as just the sort of thing that has made "increasing numbers" of Americans lose faith in the opposition. This will identify you as the spokesman for *your* party. (Other candidates on your side will scream that you're no such thing. Jealousy. Sheer jealousy.)

If the incumbent is from the other party, you can have a field day at his expense. Even if he has no desire to run again and wants only to retire and enjoy a little peace and quiet, he is fair game. His policies, naturally, can be derided, unless they happen to have been popular. But you can pick up just as many votes by selecting some personal aspect of his occupancy of the White House and sneering at *that*.

Suppose he plays croquet. Presidents have done so, and there's nothing wrong with it; in fact, there's a lot to be said for almost any diversion from the Presidential chores. But it's part of the game to assume that whatever an opposition President does is the object of stern, puritanical disapproval by the citizenry. Confide with a half-joking air to audiences here and there that if you're nominated and elected, you can promise them at least one thing: there won't be any more croquet playing in the White House. That will advance the American dream.

Make this an inflexible rule: When you tee off on the opposition, guard against a careless tendency to cite facts. You may assail the plan or the policy, as the case may be, as timid, half baked, fraught with danger, weak, dictatorial. You may object, on the one hand, that it's another case of "too little and too late" or, on the other, that its cost would be ruinous. But don't talk about names, dates or figures. You might be sorry.

All your caution may not keep you entirely out of trouble. Some people whose support you need are apt to want a little more specific information. In cozy talks with one group, to illustrate, you may remark reassuringly that you see no need for price supports on acorns. The story will get out, and the squirrel lovers will set up an aggrieved chatter. This calls for some adroit footwork. Have one of your friends say that this was a "remark made at a private dinner." Why a remark at a private dinner shouldn't reflect your true feelings has never been explained, but most people will swallow the story.

5

Any Number Can Play

". . . there ought to be practical politics."
—TULLY SCOTT, Kansas

UNTIL THE nominating convention your chief concern will be with opponents within your own party. Make it clear that you "welcome" a big field of candidates as proof that your party is not a "one-man show" and that the convention will not be a rubber-stamp proposition. After a candidate has thrown his hat into the ring with yours, avoid mention of his name in public wherever possible. If his name does come up, your reaction may be lofty, amused or indulgent.

Actually you do not ignore your opponents. Far from it.

You attack them by indirection. There is nothing to limit your feints but your own ingenuity. A few examples will suffice: Sound a warning that your party need not look for victory if it presents to the public a candidate of "limited experience." Count on your friends to point out that this is an obvious reference to Senator X, Governor Y, or General Z. Or remark sarcastically that a candidate will need more than a "pretty face" to win this year. Clearly (your friends will nod) this was a thrust at A. Again, serve notice that the voters are up in arms against "boss rule." A telling jab at Candidate B, who claims he has enough delegates in his pocket right now to snare the nomination, say your friends.

Remember your friend the gruff politician? Have him comment sagely that Candidate X made a "terrible mistake" in coming out too early, that Candidate Y missed the bus by coming out too late, that Candidate Z botched his chances by "unfortunate speeches." Your gruff politician friend may not have backed a winner since 1924, but his pronouncements will be followed with awe—and you will benefit.

The beauty of this strategy is that your opponents cannot take offense. You've mentioned no names and you are free to make a deal with any of them if he happens to beat you for the nomination.

Your opponents, of course, will be pecking away at you in the same fashion. There's a serviceable defense. Express concern lest internal quarrels leave your party "hopelessly divided" for the fight in November. Better yet, sniff that you can't stand a poor sport. Don't waste too much time on this bickering because you have bigger things to keep you busy.

For one thing, You-for-President clubs should have "sprung up" the day after you announced, if your campaign manager has been on the job. If they haven't, get a new manager now. A word about these clubs: They have no meeting places, no meetings and no bylaws, but they do have dues, and no candidate should be without them. They give an air of amateurish innocence and enthusiasm to your campaign.

As the campaign progresses, busybodies demanding facts will keep bothering you. They will want to know where you stand on such and such, what your platform will be. Don't be taken in by these diversionary tactics. Answer that you will make your views on vital issues crystal clear between now and the convention or "at the proper time." If they persist, advise them to consult your past speeches. As a sop, demand vigorous enforcement of all existing laws. Sentiment in favor of enforcing non-existing laws is almost negligible.

You will need money, there's no getting around that, and it's silly to spend your own. Announce that you want "hundreds of thousands of small contributions"—as little as $1—so that every citizen may participate in this great crusade. Toss in a dollar yourself. Declare flatly that you will accept no contributions from big corporations or labor unions. (This is safe; they're against the law.) But you will be offered some juicy contributions from all sorts of people. Take them; you can use everything you can get.

Campaign headquarters don't just grow; somebody has to pay for them. If you are one of the lucky ones who can afford the best—receptionists, tape recorders, air conditioning, the works—observe approvingly that you and your friends are "sparing no effort in this fight." A tiny mimeograph-machine–stenographer setup needs no apologies. It proves you are

running your campaign on a thrifty, no-frills, pay-as-you-go basis. Have your press agents admit, with a note of pride, that you cannot afford high-priced press agents. Remember Lincoln's Law: You can fool some of the people all the time. Which brings us to the deal.

Speeches have a place in politics. So do the homey touch, the call of duty, the general welfare. Principles have been known to influence votes. But the deal, a simple you-do-this and I'll-do-that arrangement, is something a man can get his teeth into. It produces delegates and wins nominations.

Closing a deal calls for the tiresome haggling known as a conference. The way you handle yourself at these sessions will be watched closely. At some of them you will be able to get nowhere with the other politician. He may ask more than you can give; he may be hogtied by an opponent, or he may

simply be holding out to boost his nuisance value to the opposition. Anyway, you will get nothing out of him and you'll have to make the best of it. The thing to do, as this unsatisfactory session adjourns, is to "emerge smiling broadly" with the mysterious remark that you've had a mighty interesting conversation.

Regardless of the way your deals go, your friends will pass the word, with a knowing air, that delegates are lining up for you in "impressive numbers." (Three, at this stage, may be an impressive figure to you.) Don't talk figures, except to claim several in the home states of your principal opponents. The opponents, who may know the game better than you, will worry about a double-cross. They'll claim delegates in *your* state. Better check on this.

Over in the other party, one candidate may have the nomination all sewed up. Insist that you hope he'll be nominated because you want to meet the "champ" in a chips-down contest. Have your friends explain "off the record" that he'll be the easiest man to beat in November. And as you head for the convention city, say something like this: "I wouldn't change places with any other candidate." It sounds good, means nothing.

6

Who's the Man?

". . . mistake not the fine frenzy of a Convention hall."
—L. Irving Handy, Delaware

YOU ENTER the national convention *a* candidate. Your aim is to leave it *the* candidate. To be *a* candidate you need meet only the bare, legal requirements. To persuade a convention to make you its nominee you must be good. In fact, you have got to be perfect. Without an understanding of the basic nature of a convention and its folklore you are licked before you start. Every four years entries fail through sheer ignorance.

A political convention shares the attributes of a circus, a camp meeting and an audience-participation show, with a touch of voodoo thrown in. It has its ringmaster, clowns and tightrope walkers; incantations dating back to the dim reaches of our history; spellbinding orators who hypnotize grown men and women—all leading to the choice of a winner. It has, besides, characteristics peculiarly its own. The form and details may change, but not the substance. You have but one choice: conform.

The late Senator David A. Reed of Pennsylvania, after a lifetime of attending conventions, distilled his experience down to a sentence: "Conventions," he said, "are easy on the head but hard on the feet."

Had the senator cared to, he might have added that conventions paralyze the facial muscles (constant smiling, teeth
bared, is mandatory), fray the vocal cords, ruin the digestion
and, except for the winner, the disposition. Losers sometimes
recover, but they are never the same.

Your advance man should precede you to the convention city by at least a week. There he sets up his pitch, known to the trade as your convention headquarters, staffs it with cover girls, papers the city with posters and banners, and scatters buttons, ribbons and other trinkets bearing your name by the carload lot.

He will need stacks of pamphlets containing excerpts from your speeches. Most of these will be found, in unopened cartons, by the charwomen who sweep up after you have left town. Nevertheless, order the pamphlets. It's one of the rules.

Your official campaign portrait should show you as youthful but mature, with an expression of integrity that might almost suggest grimness were it not for relieving lines of humor about the mouth. Any competent photographer can arrange this. Eyes and a pointing forefinger that seem to follow the beholder are excellent. They accustom the delegates to the suspicion that you will be a hard man to shake off.

Thwarted composers will offer you campaign songs by the bale. Refer them to your opponents and appropriate for yourself a familiar tune—one featuring the name of your state. Train your followers to whinny and roar insanely at the sound of its opening bars.

The function of your convention headquarters is to create a mood of quiet confidence that threatens at any moment to bubble over into uncontrollable jubilation. With your arrival in town, this mood ought to become almost radioactive.

You may plan to sneak into town or to be hailed by a huge reception. It must be one thing or the other. A modest welcome by a few dozen supporters will be regarded as a sign that someone planned a big one that didn't come off. That would be fatal. A rousing reception rigged by your friends is an "outpouring of loyal supporters" and a good start for your operations. Just as effective (and cheaper) is for your press agent to let it slip that you carried your own bag from the "depot" to the hotel lobby, after arriving unheralded. Of course the room clerk was shocked to see the great man carrying his own bag. The simple touch is never wasted.

After you unpack, the press agent will set up a news conference for you with reporters of the press, radio and television. They will attend, on the theory that all ratholes must be covered. Opinions on reporters differ. Some authorities hold that to treat them with common courtesy is a mark of weakness. Others recommend an approach of unabashed fawning, in the belief that reporters can "make or break" you. Choose the techniques that suit you best. You open the conference with a statement that is carefully prescribed in the rules. It goes like this:

You have been attending (or reading about) political conventions for a good many years now (more than you care to remember, ha ha), but this one is different from all the rest. Usually the delegates are out for a good time, but here you detect an atmosphere of seriousness, a sense of destiny, a realization that this convention may be the last, best hope of preserving our way of life. What this convention does may well determine whether the American people will continue to——

Here a reporter will interrupt. "Do you expect to win the nomination?" he will ask.

Stare at the questioner as if you can scarcely believe your ears. Certainly, you reply quietly. On which ballot? (Pick a number from two to five.) On the third, you predict.

This is to plant the suspicion that the result has been decided in advance and nothing remains but for the convention to go through the motions. On the first ballot, you explain patiently, the delegates will vote for their favorite sons. On the second you will forge into the lead and on the third all hands will scramble for the bandwagon.

Getting down to cases is perfectly safe at this point. When the convention is over, who'll remember?

You will be asked your views on the party platform. With one exception, don't waste time on the platform at this point. There will be one in a day or so, and you will be stuck with it. Voice confidence that your party will present a platform to which all men of good will may rally, regardless of race, creed or political affiliation.

However, you do have strong convictions on one issue (this is the exception). You will, you announce, insist on a plank pledging a "sound currency at all hazards." It is beyond the power of any agency, human or occult, to keep the sound-currency plank *out* of the platform, and since it will be in there anyway why not grab the credit? We'll return to the platform in a moment. Meanwhile, break off the conference with the press before the reporters shuffle off, yawning.

7

The Man Who

"There stands one man taller than all the rest."
—Patrick A. Collins, Massachusetts

Aconvention is a costly affair and, to get its money's worth, the party will want to drag it out to at least a five-day stand. This involves the frequent billing of coloraturas, Irish tenors and elder statesmen to keep the show on its feet. (They say television will change all this. They said the crossbow would end warfare, too.) Anyway, these fillers give you extra time and you will need every minute of it.

For contrast to your own appearance of unassuming, good-humored confidence, flog your headquarters into a bedlam of purposeful bustling. Photoflashes, bleary-eyed typists, jangling telephones—that sort of thing. Delegates must be lured in with the relentless progress of a column of ants, and your staff must exchange knowing looks as each group departs. The visiting delegates, presumably, have pledged their support to you. In order to bring them in, free beer and sandwiches will work wonders.

By now it will be dawning on some of the younger delegates that their leaders expect them to take orders. Cash in on their disillusionment with a sharp warning that this convention will not be "bossed." You may pick up a vote or two.

For your own part, you say, you have made no deals and will make none. This is especially important if you have your eye on the Vice Presidential nomination.

Let us consider the Vice Presidency for a moment. The pay is good, the expense account generous. It offers social prestige and opportunity for advancement. The working conditions are pleasant, the hours short, the responsibilities few and the duties agreeable. All in all, these points add up to the desirable employment, and the country has had no difficulty in hiring Vice Presidents. Someone will ask if you care to apply. Since the main requirement is being on the opposite side from the Presidential nominee on all big issues, you may turn out to be fully qualified. If you'd like the job, snort contemptuously that you are not interested in second place on the ticket. The roster of Vice Presidents is full of names of those who, as the conventions opened, were "not interested."

With similar disdain, report that various "Stop You" movements are being engineered but will get nowhere. The other candidates have troubles of their own, but the implication that they are ganging up on you suggests they fear you as the big threat. Also, it may be worth a certain amount of pro-underdog support.

As news breaks that one delegation has switched to an opponent, comment with a hearty "A man is known by the company he keeps." If you snare a hatful of votes, hint mysteriously that this is only a superficial symptom of deep, hidden forces that may break surface at any moment. Check on the arrangements for your spontaneous demonstration.

The spontaneous demonstration is to the political convention what nuclear fission is to the A-bomb. It is the explosion of accumulated, won't-take-no-for-an-answer demand that you run for President, triggered by the magic of your name being placed in nomination and fed by a chain reaction of noise and motion. The spontaneous demonstration, obviously, is no self-generated phenomenon; it requires painstaking preparation.

Arming your delegates and alternates with horns, squawkers, cowbells, flags and posters is, of course, standard operating procedure. Brass bands are cheap, considering the stakes, and the convention-hall organist will set the house to vibrating like a gong for a slight additional charge. However, unscrupulous politicians acting for other candidates will do the same thing. What you want is the most demonstrative and spontaneous demonstration of spontaneity ever presented.

The secret lies in simple staff planning. Fix it with the local political boss to pack the galleries with You-for-President fans. No others admitted. A clapping, stomping, chanting gallery not only beefs up your own demonstration but its boos can reduce the opposition to hopeless frustration. You may have to come right out and admit your friendship with the local boss in order to get his help. Proclaim (don't admit) that you are delighted to join forces with this stalwart party captain in the interests of the American people.

There is just one catch. Some other candidate may have reached the boss first. In that case, salvage what you can with a shocked denunciation of the unholy alliance between the other candidate and the machine politician and assure the public that the delegates will not submit to steam-roller tactics or mob rule. In resorting to such shabby tactics the "other camp" is betraying its fear.

Speaking of fear, your own political courage must be beyond dispute, and a dramatic sample of it, just before the voting starts, does no harm. By this time, you will recall, the convention will have adopted the party platform. For your courage trick you must pick a plank. Almost any plank will do. Let's assume you take the one on corruption. The plank will pledge the party to an unrelenting drive against corruption in government, or words to that effect.

Now, at the proper time, the man you choose for the task will be recognized to deliver the nominating, or Man Who, speech. Before he does so, he announces that he has just received from you (you are not in the convention hall, according to Rule One of convention etiquette) a telegram which you have asked him to read.

You have studied the platform with great interest, the telegram will state, and heartily endorse every word of it. But in all candor you must clarify your position on one point so there may be no misunderstanding before the delegates undertake their solemn duty to nominate a man for the Presidency.

You note that the platform calls for a campaign against corruption in government. As you interpret this phrase, it means in *or out* of government, and if you become President you will act on this interpretation.

It's as simple as that. The impact of the trick, if it is properly executed, will be uncanny. Your friends stare at one another in stunned admiration. When, their expressions will ask, has the world witnessed such incredible, raw courage? Your sense of honor has impelled you to utter naked frankness at the risk of losing the Presidency itself!

With that out of the way, your man may begin the nominating speech. The classic Man Who speech is a highly stylized literary form in which structure is everything, content nothing. Its opening "we meet here today" passage leads naturally to a graceful reference to the convention city where our pioneer forefathers faced peril with courage, initiative, self-reliance and a neighborly concern for their fellow men. This easily suggests the type of leadership for which the country is pleading today.

The speaker knows the man to answer the call, a man who is a product of modern America, who was not reared in the lap of luxury, who has labored with his hands, a man who has earned a wage and met a payroll, who knows that public office is a public trust, a man who pledges performance, not promises, a man who will be deaf to the preachments of despair, a man who . . .

The crowd knows that the speaker will nominate you. He knows they know it. Yet neither side betrays the other. As the orator dangles clue after tantalizing clue to your identity before the audience, they wriggle in a delicious agony of suspense. The effect can be beguiling to the spectator, soul-satisfying to the participants.

At last, no longer able to contain his secret, the speaker surrenders. His lips form the name of "the man who will be next President of the United States." You! But the words are lost in the roar of the spontaneous demonstration.

Right here, modern science could conceivably undermine politics as we know it. The demonstration is going out over television, and the image of the old-time convention war horse, a sweaty 300-pounder, cavorting in the aisles with your picture on a pole may have questionable vote appeal on a 27-inch screen. Keep him in the background for sound effects and steer your younger female delegates into camera range.

Try to maneuver things so that your demonstration will be the first of the convention. That way it will appear fresh to the delegates who have not seen one for four years. The demonstrations of the second and succeeding candidates suffer from the handicap of having to follow. If your demonstration cannot be the first, it must be the longest. The convention chairman may try to limit all demonstrations to the same length. Refuse to be intimidated by a gavel. Experts time these affairs by the clock on the theory that the more protracted the uproar the better the candidate. (It may be as good a way as any to judge.)

Next come the seconding speeches. They are a dull interlude, dreaded by the audience but cherished by the speakers, to whom they offer a mention in the official convention record and a chance to strut their stuff before the television viewers back home. Humor them; the day is coming when every vote will count.

At long last the convention is ready to get down to the real business, the voting for the party's nominee. The delegates will be in a state of profound convention shock, yearning for a cool shower and bed. Someone is sure to suggest that the balloting be postponed until tomorrow. Don't let him get away with it. By morning wiser counsel may prevail and spoil everything.

Well, you've made it (we'll say). And now, according to a quaint custom, the convention will ask itself: "But will he take the nomination? Will he accept?" The query is your cue to step out of the wings for the first time.

You needn't keep the meeting on tenterhooks for long. Treat yourself to the last flat, unqualified statement you'll be permitted to make for weeks to come: "I accept the nomination."

You do so on sober reflection, with a deep sense of humility (we're back to that again) and responsibility. Your nomination is proof that this great nation sets no limits on the heights to which a citizen may aspire. In return for this great honor the party has bestowed on you, here and now you pledge your utmost energies in the coming campaign to present the issues to the voters without fear, rancor or resort to weasel words. You invite not only the members of your own party but right-thinking Americans of all political faiths to enlist under your banner. With the party's nominee for Vice President as your running mate, you are confident of victory. He and you will make an "unbeatable team."

Possibly, if you have skimmed through these chapters, attempted short cuts or ignored their lessons, you have lost. Send the winner a telegram pledging your "wholehearted support" and slink home. Four years is not a long time, and you may get a second chance. And start over again on page 1.

8

Put Your Background to Work

"The lesson at the mother's knee . . ."
—HARRY S. EDWARDS, Georgia

A s YOUR party's nominee for President you will be many things, but you won't be lonely. Your immediate family, parents, distant relatives—even long-dead ancestors—will be constant companions. You will be held strictly accountable for them. Hastily thrown together, this company can be merely a ragtag band of camp followers who will embarrass you at every turn. A little foresight, careful selection and intensive indoctrination can weld them into an elite corps, capable of carrying its share of the load, and more. Equip them with a fascinating outline of your early life and struggles, and, so far as background is concerned, you are in business.

Your ancestors must be of "sturdy" American stock, in this country for several generations. At least one grandfather should have been a veteran of the Civil War, and if he wasn't it isn't too late to draft him. Either the Confederate or Union side is acceptable, but in the latter case detach him from Sherman's army. The South remembers. One grandfather in blue, the other in gray is ideal, and if you can arrange this you get perfect marks on ancestors.

Whatever your parents were, you owe them everything. From your mother you learned neighborliness and a sense of duty; your father taught you the joys of hard work and how to plow a straight furrow. Even one alert, surviving parent in the nineties gives you an almost indecent advantage over your opponent. These elderly parties have a knack for turning up the most quotable quotes of the campaign.

Your background (early American stock) implies no lack of respect or admiration for post-Mayflower Americans. Their numbers are impressive and you must be unstinting in your praise of other nationalities. You may skip the Russians.

A family album is almost as essential to the campaign as a mimeograph machine. It should be edited well in advance to cull out the unflattering snapshots. A studio portrait of you at the age of two is, of course, indispensable. You will be amazed how many voters will read into that empty little face the signs of future greatness.

Pictures of you in family groups will show that you were not a "loner," and the athletic theme may be developed by shots of you on the high-school baseball team. Any other team may be substituted, obviously, except chess or fencing. If your high-school graduation picture is available, complete with an uncanny prophecy of your man-of-destiny future, haul it out. Should the book disclose that you were known as "stinky" or "pinhead," buy up all copies you can lay your hands on and burn them.

Background material prepared by your staff should describe you as just an "average student" in school. It should explain that with your native ability your marks would have been excellent, but, "like all kids," you neglected your studies for more robust pursuits. This scotches the suspicion that you may have been just plain stupid and builds you up as the average, non-bookish American boy.

The opposition will stop at nothing, and if it can dig up your school records, showing disgustingly high marks in black and white, you must counter at once. Start the legend that it was you who hoisted the dean's nightshirt on the flagpole. (Even by your late teens you probably had outgrown such nonsense, but that is not the point.) Let your staff give out the bare details. Plenty of classmates will confirm the story and embroider it into one of the great sagas of your university.

On the practical side, pass the word that, as a student, you took charge of the club or fraternity as it was about to go on into bankruptcy and within three months had transformed it into the Fort Knox of the Pan-Hellenic Council. To say nothing of the time you managed your roommate's campaign for class treasurer, displaying a combination of youthful idealism and political shrewdness that completely routed the entrenched opposition. In brief, play down the brains angle and stress the high-spirited, go-getter aspects of your schooling.

(Since those days, of course, your naturally active and inquisitive mind has matured and new acquaintances invariably express wonderment at your broad range of knowledge. To achieve this reaction, add zing to your conversations with remarks like this: "It's interesting to note that 160 years after Benjamin Franklin invented the bifocal lens in 1780, Russia was spending 183,955,000,000 rubles a year." Any cheap almanac has a million of them.)

In Lincoln's day it was a distinct advantage for a candidate to come from a poor family. This is no longer the case; the public has grown more tolerant in recent years. But don't overdo it. If your family is immoderately wealthy, have your publicity staff whittle down its holdings to a decent level. Probably a good compromise is a family that is sound, hard-working and prosperous. The key word is "hard-working." Whatever your background, you know what hard work means. It may take a little ingenuity, but by some twist—an eccentric father is one possibility—your upbringing must have taught you the meaning of hard work. The details could be tiresome, but in its broad outlines the matter is pretty much one you can control.

9

Put Your Wife to Work

*"Women are the expression of God's tenderest benef-
icence to men."*
—JOHN S. RHEA, Kentucky

THE EXTENT to which you can control your wife is debatable—and critical. You may find yourself wishing you had been a little more foresighted when you married. Perhaps, at the time, you *did* have some hope that she'd be an asset in a campaign and it didn't work out. Time does strange things to women. Well, you have a wife and must make the most of her. She will be a campaign issue of a peculiarly subtle sort. Your job is to make sure that basically she is in the great tradition of the Candidate's Wife.

Fundamental No. 1 is that she does not want you to run. Being a woman, and realistic, she doubtless will rebel at such a preposterous notion. Remind her that, in the interest of the greater good, you are running not from choice but out of a sense of duty. Same with your wife. Her every impulse is to stay home with your family in her accustomed, comfortable surroundings. The White House has no attraction for her; she recoils at the thought. But she must be a "good sport" and go along.

Fundamental No. 2 is that you always "consult" her on major problems. Her views on wordly affairs may be naïve or worthless, but you would not dream of taking an important step without seeking her advice. Women love to think that women have sagacity to spare, and your consulting your wife puts you on record as endorsing this harmless fiction.

Fundamental No. 3 is affection, working both ways. Your wife is not permitted to go out of the house without the orchid that is her badge of womanly attraction for you. The daily orchid may slip your mind; be safe and have her place a standing order. The story, however, is that "he (you) never forgets." Every woman in the country will be asking her husband why *he* can't be like you. The result will be the loss of some husband votes, but the wives will more than make up for them.

The other sort of affection—your wife's for you—is completely different. You are asking the voters to trust you to make decisions that may affect their jobs, their pocketbooks, their very lives. Your wife, though, must treat you as a careless six-year-old, explaining with amused resignation that she always has to remind you to wear your rubbers, to wipe your feet on the door mat and to change to a new necktie. This is for public consumption, remember, and the voters will want visible evidence to support your wife's testimony. She may supply this in many ways, whenever she is sure people are slyly observing her: straightening out your coat collar, adjusting your handkerchief and removing a bit of lint from your lapel. Remind her to carry a spare length of thread for this purpose.

Under this same general rule, your wife must be prepared to retail the story of your courtship, and it had better be a sensationally average romance. She was the girl next door, who didn't like you at first but fell head over heels in love with you when you grew up. Or your parents were friends and tried to promote the match, which produced the inevitable balking and finally love.

Your wife need not go into details, and if you first met as blind dates in a beer joint she may gloss over the story a trifle. There is enough drabness in people's lives. When they read the papers they want entertainment. The publication of your love affair, incredible as it may seem to you and your intimates, is a phase of democracy at work.

As we have pointed out, your wife need not meet every last specification for the ideal campaign partner. A handsome wife makes it nice for you, but unless she is spectacularly ill-favored her face is not likely to become a campaign issue. Other women, for one thing, are likely to warm up to a wife who isn't too attractive. What's more to the point is whether your wife is the homebody or clubwoman type. In extreme cases the former may be downright ignorant of what's going on around her. The civic-leader-type woman,

on the other hand, is apt not only to have opinions on every conceivable problem but also an irrepressible urge to express them. This type can be tricky to handle. If it represents your problem you realize by now that it must be tackled gingerly. It might be wise to tell her, if you dare, to put her opinions in the deep freeze for the duration. She should be expressing her homemaker qualities. If she hasn't any, she can keep busy developing a few.

The housewife type is, on the whole, safer but not fool-proof. Voters like to think that the First Lady will enliven official functions with something more scintillating than tales of the new dishwasher and how sick she is of peanut-butter sandwiches. The impression you are striving for is that your wife, while essentially a home-lover, is pretty acute about the bigger things. Prime her with a few observations (nice, safe ones) on the more obvious current "situations." If she has a flair for that sort of thing she may emerge from the campaign with a reputation for a penetrating wit and a pretty taste for epigram.

This will be particularly effective if she has announced, right off the bat, that she isn't going to "break her rule against making speeches." Up to then, nobody had heard of it, but the idea is to say it as if this suddenly invented canon has all the sanctity of a decision by the Supreme Court.

There are just a few more points which apply to all wives. One is that she must be a "gracious hostess." A few months in this kind of work will have taught your wife to keep her true feelings about your associates in this great cause to herself; otherwise, hire somebody to show her the ropes. A candidate had better be a bachelor than have a wife who cannot be called, with some degree of plausibility, a "gracious hostess."

Finally, a word on recipes. Your wife must be alerted to disclose the formula for preparing one of your favorite dishes. It must not be a *cordon bleu* confection; some simple item for Sunday-night supper is much the best. Research indicates that a sound, all-purpose recipe is one of the variations of scrambled eggs. For reasons that space does not permit us to analyze, it is considered noteworthy and a sign that the Republic will be in safe hands if the candidate eats scrambled eggs.

If you care to bother, you may cast a lure for the male-cook vote, using one of *your* favorite recipes for bait. Here the standards are turned upside down. Your recipe must be incredibly complicated, calling for endless chopping, shredding and simmering, and exotic, hard-to-obtain condiments. In the rush of the campaign, nobody will have the time to test it out to your possible discredit.

Whether your wife accompanies you on your campaign trips is for her to decide. You might be able to force her—we wouldn't know about that—but you don't want her tagging along like a resentful slave girl. As a willing companion she is a valuable example of the wife who will go anywhere with her man. If she'll have none of it, the public explanation is that her post is at home with the children. When in doubt, apply the basic rule of politics: a little of both.

10

Put the Kiddies to Work

"He must have a private life . . ."
—Charles E. Littlefield, Maine

CHILDREN—you might as well face it—are a gamble. Voters will draw all sorts of significant conclusions about your personal and domestic life from your children—how many, how old and, especially, how they behave. To an even greater extent than is the case with your wife, you are stuck with your children for better or worse, and it is up to you to see that it is no worse than necessary.

Some candidates have grandchildren. There's no point in trying to conceal this. If you are old enough to have grandchildren, that fact will be public property. The grandchildren themselves can be recruited for campaign duty. Show you are fond of the little ones. A well-publicized visit to their house is sure to produce pictures of you greeting the youngsters and hoisting them on your shoulder. You might let it be known that you've served time as a baby sitter for the kiddies. This takes care of several helpful aspects of your personality: the big man taking time out to be human, love of children and a desire to help out harried young parents. Not a bad haul from a brace of grandchildren.

Getting back to your own offspring—very young ones are best. They are evidence that you are young yourself. But here again is something most candidates are lax about. If you have no young children it is probably too late now to do anything about it.

Adolescent boys are practically a dead loss. You may have one or two and be fond of them. During the campaign, however, they will be studied objectively. Keep them under wraps as much as possible; they are particularly annoying to photographers. Send them to camp, if possible. Meanwhile, your publicity staff should be circulating the story that you and the boys are "pals." No matter how busy you are, you find time for father-and-son fishing trips. This does not mean that you indulge them. They have to earn their own spending money. They too are learning the meaning of hard work.

Young girls, unless they are unbearably homely, are an asset from start to finish. If you are thus blessed, take them along on campaign trips. Where you will have to pretend to enjoy yourself, they will be having the time of their lives. Shell out money to make them more attractive than ever. Play the doting, indulgent father. Be seen sharing little jokes with them. Your chances of getting your picture in papers and magazines will increase tremendously if you can pair up with a good-looking daughter.

A judicious hint of possible romance for marriage-age daughters is called for. The girl, of course, need not commit herself; her job is to allude to the possibility of a White House wedding, which may appeal to her and is sure to please the feminine electorate.

Older children demand cautious treatment. If you have a boy of draft age, make it clear that "he must take his chances with the rest."

Unless your children are too young to talk there is one trick that never misses. Your children are naturally intrigued about the possibility of living in the White House. So, at the proper time in the campaign, mention that you've talked the whole thing over with them. The surface appeal of this evidence that you let half-grown children help you reach important decisions is hard to explain, but it's there all the same.

You (however) are well aware of the effect of all this public attention on your children, you declare. It is one of the penalties that go with answering the call to duty. Whatever else happens, you say, you are not going to permit your children to get big heads if you are elected. (This could well be the most ridiculous statement of your campaign, but it won't sound so at the time.)

11

Put Your Home Town to Work

". . . we ask what his neighbors say about him."
—Paul Jones, Arkansas

PRESS RELEASES and well-planned sidelights sponsored by your relatives and friends will help publicize your background. There's a better way, though, a sort of pageant of the influences which have made you the simple, honest, forthright, successful man you are today and a logical choice for President. It is called the Visit Home, and it should be presented very soon after your nomination when many voters, for the first time, awaken to the fact that they've got to make up their minds about you.

Possibly you have not the faintest desire to go back to the old home town. You may have sworn forty years ago that if ever you had the chance to break out, nothing could drag you back to the dreary place. Now, you will find, things look different. You probably have a normal impulse to confront the elders who prophesied that you'd come to no good end. Here's the chance to obey it and pick up votes on the side.

The home-town-revisited project enables you, in one shrewd move, to expand your vote-getting territory tremendously. Say you are now living in the West. Your home town, or your wife's, or your mother's, will then happen to be in the East. Or, if you are operating on the Atlantic seaboard, you may claim, for what it's worth, to be a native son, or related to a native son of the West. Politically, it is possible to be in two places at once.

This show must be produced lavishly, and fortunately you are now working on the party's expense account. Meticulous advance planning is vital. Nothing must be left to chance. Every action, word or gesture has its meaning and purpose. Space does not permit discussion of each detail and refinement. Here we can cite only a few examples for your guidance.

First, it is desirable to arrive either by train or in an open automobile. The local airport, if there is any, is likely to be either hot and dusty or ankle-deep in mud. However you arrive, with the new supermarket, the new post office and the elimination of the old grade crossing, you won't recognize your old birthplace. Shake hands with the reception committee and declare brightly, "It hasn't changed a bit."

The visit will do wonders for your ego, too, because you will be pleased to note that while you have been maturing into vigorous prime of life, your contemporaries have been growing old, fat and bald. The chairman, of course, will nudge your memory on names and you hail each man with a jovial "I'd recognize you anywhere." Women get a roguish "Prettier than ever."

A good part of this visit will be devoted to calls prescribed as rigidly as anything outside of naval etiquette. Drop in to see "Doc," the druggist who gave you your first job. He'll give reporters a fill-in on the time you ate yourself sick on banana splits. Ferret out an old crone whom you present to your wife as "the prettiest girl in town" or, if that's too far-fetched, the "best cook."

Look up the school principal (you will have planted the legend that you were once expelled for some boyish prank) and have him recount the tale with a "twinkle in his eye." All he'll want for this slight service is an invitation to the White House.

When the program has fallen behind schedule, but not before, stop everything to visit your favorite schoolteacher. She will be elderly, in retirement now, but with the same caustic schoolroom manner overlaying her keen intelligence and motherly affection. Where others have been fawning on you, she will snap and address you as Tom, Dick or Harry, volunteering some pointed advice on how to "behave when you get down there in Washington."

Listen to this advice soberly and guffaw immoderately at her other comments. The chairman, who wants to get on with the program, will be fidgeting, but your wife can tell him you just lose all track of time when you're talking with old friends. As you break away from the teacher, she can recall to reporters that you were a bright lad, mischievous but without a mean bone in your body.

Somewhere, fit in a call on the local sage. Remark that his sort of common-sense thinking is what we need in the government. He will not dispute this.

This should leave time for a run out to the Old Barton Place, where you used to go swimming when you played hooky. Your shocked comments at the way this property has been allowed to run down should be audible to everyone. It's an outrage, you protest, that the government has done nothing to preserve these historic old sites.

Some scholars believe that the home-town visit should end with a speech. Others favor a few words ending with "This is where I feel at home; you are my kind of folks."

Then shove off. With luck you won't have to come back for years.

The pattern outlined above will serve equally well for a visit to your wife's home town. Counting relatives and ancestors scattered about the country, the resourceful candidate will be able to visit home towns in almost every doubtful state in the Union.

12

Do It Yourself

"... *the plain, blunt, honest citizen* ..."
—LEON ABBETT, New Jersey

THE TRAGEDY of the Presidential also-ran might be summed up in the epitaph "He didn't understand." Many a candidate has skimmed the preliminary hurdles with a graceful *grand jeté en tournant* only to botch the main event—the campaign itself—with a ludicrous pratfall. Usually the cause is obvious: misdirected planning based on a false premise. It is remarkable, considering the mass of evidence to the contrary, how the superstition persists that the function of a campaign is to enlighten the voters on the issues. For you as a citizen to entertain this notion speaks highly of your decency and idealism. As a candidate, you must reject it as a dangerous conceit; otherwise your plunge into politics will be a swan dive into an empty pool.

A campaign is not a Great Debate. It is a Big Build-up. Its objective is to present you as the Presidential beau ideal, the average man in spades, doubled. By election day you must become, if you are not already, as typically American as the home run, with common sense, a keen but inoffensive intelligence, and simple tastes in food, clothes, art and literature. A man of red blood, sincerity and a touch, but no more, of human frailty. You have yet to meet the man you don't like, and you want everybody to be happy. You are fond of animals, children, your wife and registered voters.

These and other aspects of your character may be highlighted by dialogue that glimmers, sparkles and scorches, by clever bits of stage business and a commanding presence to illustrate your personality and your attitude toward things, ideas and people. With proper direction you will be able to give a creditable performance with a good deal less native talent than a Barrymore.

The comparison with Barrymore is not so farfetched as it might sound. Politics, after all, is just a phase of show business. As a candidate you will be in the movies, starring in one- or two-minute productions to be sandwiched into the daily television schedule, somewhere between Captain Video and Howdy Doody.

In your film role you will play yourself. The only other character, the classic "Citizen," will be portrayed by a depressingly average man or woman who asks you questions. They will be searching queries such as, "Do you favor honesty in public office?" or "Do you think we should outlaw hurricanes?" Your answers—crisp, terse and fearless—are the fattest part of the dialogue. It is up to you to speak your lines with authority and a disarming candor.

This technique will stamp you as a man on top of every situation, never at a loss, with nothing to hide. That, remember, is the keynote of your whole campaign. The farce may make you writhe inwardly; you might prefer the stimulus of matching wits with a set of seasoned hecklers. Don't tinker with the system. People still love to see the ball knocked out of the park even if it's been lobbed up to the plate by the batting-practice pitcher.

And speaking of show business, there's live television. Properly utilized, it can sharpen up for the viewers the picture you're trying to present—You as the embodiment of all they yearn for—the guy who will make their lives more gracious, their breath sweeter, their take-home pay larger and their attractions more irresistible.

In the circumstances, of course, you can't be natural on television. You'll be in the hands of advertising men and women, displaced movie directors and interior decorators. They'll insist on the homey touch and you might as well go along; it seems to work.

For your television appearance you'll be seated comfortably—and don't fidget—before a plywood backdrop of a fireplace or bookcases, or perhaps a symbolic scene such as the Washington Monument, the Lincoln Memorial or a sweeping panorama of fields of waving grain. In this cozy setting you talk simply with your viewers, man-to-man or man-to-woman, and you'd better lay off the orator's tricks and exude sincerity.

Make-up men will assist this illusion with their peculiar artistry. Malelike, you may shudder when they first apply their creams, eyebrow pencil and tinted powder to your weather-beaten face, but you'll get used to it—you'll be surprised how quickly. Have you never heard of the lure of grease paint?

To help you really live your part, your press agents will have composed a whole cycle of tales relating to the "early you." There are, for example, those boyhood jobs every candidate must have had, or must invent. They should be reminiscent of an earlier, simpler period, such as the small-town lad working for the local creamery, the little merchant delivering newspapers, the gawky youngster wrestling sugar barrels in the general store.

It should be no trouble for your public-relations consultant to locate a former employer who will remember you as a fun-loving youth, fond of a practical joke but with it all a willing, dependable worker who moved up steadily to more responsible tasks. The implication is plain: Just as you climbed from errand boy to grocery clerk, you are now progressing from whatever you are to the Presidency of the United States, in a kind of inexorable fulfillment.

It will be well to establish an interest in public men and affairs dating back to your childhood. You may recall the treasured experience when, as a boy, you heard, say, Theodore Roosevelt speak. (He's a good one, acceptable to both parties.) You don't remember what he said, of course; perhaps, boylike, you fell asleep, but it was a memorable occasion just the same. Since thousands of your contemporaries also heard T. R. it doesn't mean much, but still it will sound like fate, or something, to many of the younger voters.

Bear in mind that you stand pledged to wage a vigorous campaign. If you made this promise lightly, you will soon discover your error. From now until the polls open you must comport yourself like a human vitamin generator. Your back will creak, your head will throb and invisible devils will broil your feet with blowtorches. But in every public appearance —and "public" in this context means in the presence of all except members of your immediate family and one or two trusted intimates—you will bounce jauntily.

A rough rule is that the less jaunty you feel, because of age, overindulgence or long hours, the more jauntily you must behave. Voters are understandably disenchanted by the sight of a sagging, listless candidate. A display of brisk, locked-in energy may be supplemented by appropriate support from your staff. Instruct them to "admit" to reporters that you run them ragged. A nightmarish schedule that wilts them like soda-counter lettuce braces you to the crispness of iced celery. Local politicians who hoist themselves aboard your campaign special should be invited to chime in. As partial payment for the free ride they'll be glad to comment enviously on your vigor. Late at night you may collapse and let a professional prize-fight trainer slap and thump the aches away.

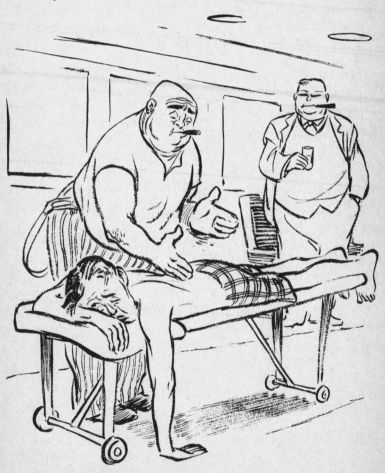

Your resistance to physical strain and discomfort may be proved by a ride in a convertible, top down, during a cloudburst. Wave to the onlookers with your battered campaign hat (an assistant should batter one for you) and let the rains descend. Knowing enough to come in out of the rain is considered one of the more rudimentary intelligence tests. It does not apply to candidates. Some unappreciative reporter will inquire what in the world you were thinking of. You reply (simply): "These people came out to see me; it was the least I could do."

For most of the campaign you will be the very personi-fication of smiling, unruffled affability, but the picture must be rounded out. Once—only once—plan to lose your temper publicly. Some remark of your opponent may be taken to go "so far beyond the bounds of decent American principles of fair play" that you blow your top. Perhaps a tomato is fired at you and splatters your wife. The cause is not impor-tant; adverse musical criticism has served this purpose. The point is that you get into the record that you can be pushed so far; then you react like any other red-blooded American.

The luxury of losing your temper during a campaign can easily become a habit, though. The so-called "oaths" that are acceptable to the public are not very satisfying, but you'd better limit yourself to "By golly," "Gee," and "Son-of-a-gun." In theory, at least, the voter will sanction nothing stronger.

A badge of courage never hurt a candidate and you should keep your eyes open for a chance to snag one. The back-firing of an automobile in your neighborhood may be worked up into a respectable little shooting scare that panicked every member of your party—except you, who remained calm and amused. A fire within a half-mile radius naturally "threatens" the hotel where you are staying. Act accordingly.

"He [meaning you] personally supervised plans to evacu-ate the hotel, but fortunately the precaution proved un-necessary," your press agent might confide to reporters.

13

Just Folks

"In all these things you are the typical American."
—JOHN M. THURSTON, Nebraska

Y OU WILL be judged, fairly or not, by your attitude toward things, concrete and abstract, your opinions on every conceivable phase of human activity. As a candidate you are public property and have forfeited the tolerance you could have demanded as a private citizen.

Let us illustrate: You are, we'll say, a minor authority on the French Impressionists. Sometime in your campaign you will fall into the clutches of a culture-happy group and be dragged into an art museum. A moment's contemplation of a Toulouse-Lautrec or a Renoir would refresh your soul. And it would be fatal.

For one thing, this is an age of nationalism. Why link yourself in the public mind with foreign-sounding names? There is a safe formula for eluding the snare. Ignore the canvases until you spot a well-known work like "Washington Crossing the Delaware" or "Custer's Last Stand." Plant yourself before it reverently. Admit, in an aside, that you can't "make heads or tails out of this modern stuff." Then get out before you blurt something heartfelt and, therefore, unwise.

Your approach to literary criticism may be equally forth-right. Your press agents will reveal that you are a voracious reader of history and biography and for relaxation enjoy nothing better than a good detective story. If you have the time you may want to read such a book and keep it in view for display purposes. Novels are out. Publishers can't keep up with the demand for readable novels, but for a candidate they arouse only suspicion and distrust. One more thing: no comic books.

The litmus-paper test of a candidate's unswerving Americanism is baseball. Wisely, the campaign has been timed to coincide with the World Series. Don't schedule public appearances while the games are going on. It would be useless, anyway. Be intensely concerned about the progress of each game. Whenever you pass a radio or television set inquire anxiously, "What's the score?" If you're a little hazy on who's playing, get briefed on it. A mistaken reference to what player is on which team could shatter public confidence in you.

Baseball, politically speaking, is a spectator sport. Fishing is something else again. You must be seen fishing and must give every evidence of enjoying the pastime. (You can, at least, be sure of *catching* fish. A friendly game warden will gladly overstock a section of stream until a number of fish take your hook just to escape the crowd.) There is no explaining the dogma that men who seek the Presidency must be ardent anglers. Voters who could not bait a hook insist on candidates who fish. You can only submit.

This too will pass. Inescapably your travels will take you to national and local shrines. Assuming that your staff has coached you to avoid the obvious boners about which shrine you are in at the moment, you will find that these trips can be worth their cost in boredom and sore feet. As you enter, settle your features in a "solemn mien." If invited to sit on a chair once occupied by Franklin Pierce, for in-

stance, or Millard Fillmore, decline "gravely." You are sensitive to the honor, your manner will stress, but you have a deep reverence for the past and the nation's heroes and would not presume to associate yourself, even remotely, with the giants of history.

The same need for restraint, you will find, will run through your campaign like a symphonic theme. There is liquor. What, where and how much you drink as a private tax-payer is pretty much your own business. As a candidate, you are not permitted to decide the question for yourself and your ulcer. Your public-relations man should set the record straight on your alcoholic habits. One cocktail is your standard, "never more than two." You dilute your whisky with branch water. In public, however, confine your campaign drinking to cider, lemonade, milk or buttermilk. Make a show of consuming this stuff, sustained by the knowledge that eventually a friend will take you aside for a jolt of 100-proof as a chaser.

The man whose appetite revolts at the sight of huge quantities of food is, to all practical purposes, disqualified as a Presidential possibility. The truth is that the seeker after high office is expected to eat his way through a campaign. At hot-dog roasts, clambakes and barbecues, the candidate must not only eat immoderately, but must do so "with relish." Other persons may stuff themselves without attracting undue attention; when a candidate does, it's a sign of robust good health, an unaffected liking for plain food and a steady character. The diet will vary with the geography. Fried chicken, corn bread and black-eyed peas will be spread before you in the South, fish chowder in New England, scrapple in Pennsylvania, barbecued steer in the West. Clean up your plate (with relish).

So that your eating may embrace more political subdivisions, pass the word that you send to Vermont every year for maple syrup, to Wisconsin for cheese and have friends in Idaho who ship you potatoes. (Maine either is yours or it isn't, depending on which party you're in, so don't worry about the Maine-Idaho potato feud.) Possibly your own state prides itself on a particular delicacy; enter into a good-natured debate with somebody on the relative merits of your state's product and his. Loyalty to his state is still considered good form for a candidate.

As you eat, don't forget the campaign amenities. Praise "these good women" who prepared the viands on which you nearly gagged.

14

Grass Roots

"If you knew how many good things I had to say . . ."
—JAMES A. McKENZIE, Kentucky

TO PRAISE, in fact, will become second nature to you as the crusade wears on, and your approbation will blanket people, their relatives, domestic pets and livestock. Sophistication is no more becoming to the candidate than it would be to Alice in Wonderland, and your discovery of laudable qualities at every turn will label you as a man of artless simplicity.

Perhaps you have been taking it for granted that when you ride a train or an airplane somebody runs it, somebody sells the tickets, somebody handles your baggage. That's how they earn their livings. On a campaign trip such services become personal favors which leave you almost—but not quite—speechless with gratitude. Thank the engineer or the pilot profusely for their splendid work. Thank the conductor, the porter, everyone connected with the operation. The

same applies to waiters, clerks, newsboys and so on. Thank any stewardesses, without leering. Upon dining in a restaurant, go back to the kitchen and thank the chef—but refer to him as the cook. When you have been assigned a police escort, ignore the fact that the officers have been serving under orders and express appreciation all around. Praise of a more practical sort, in the form of a $10 bill per man, is an acceptable substitute for eloquence.

In your contacts with working men you'll have a chance to parade your deep-rooted sympathy with labor. It may be that somewhere along the line, on a summer job or before you entered politics, you've picked up a union card. Display it, a treasured memento, at appropriate intervals. Candidates without union cards of their own have, in the past, hit on the alternative of alluding to "union cards in my family." They may be referring to a brother-in-law who *had* to join a union to land a job, but as a device for associating oneself with labor it's better than nothing.

Children, other than your own, will be thrust at you at awkward moments. Baby kissing is coming to be considered crude, but children still rate a warm reception. They will be voters someday; their parents are now. Curb your impatience.

Frequently, especially in towns where your party controls the courthouse, kids will be let out of school to watch your campaign party parade down Main Street. The treat will put them in a good humor and their numbers can help swell a disappointing turn-out into a "great outpouring." You may take credit for the holiday "laughingly." Make it a point to thank the local high-school band for showing up to greet you. Only those directly concerned need know about your $50 contribution to the band's uniform fund.

Invariably, candidates give "scoops" to 11-year-old editors. Although the attention makes the editors insufferable to their friends and families, you'd better co-operate. You'll get letters from plenty of these pushy little characters. Pick one out, preferably from a state where your campaign needs prodding, and reply to the juvenile journalist, slipping in a modest item of news.

Don't waste a really juicy story on the boy; the reporters covering your campaign might resent it. If the item is trivial enough, though, the reporters will go along with the gag. Everybody will be satisfied. The 11-year-old gets his scoop, the professionals get a side story for a dull day and you get credit for being kind to children.

Where there are children there will be dogs. A judiciously patted dog can make all the difference in a doubtful ward. Recall little anecdotes about your own dog, letting your voice drop huskily if he has passed on. Cats are something else. There are those who resent a cat's independence and claim, moreover, that a liking for cats is effeminate. Cats, being controversial subjects, should be avoided.

With any kind of luck animals should present no problem. This is not true of people, particularly those with brains. Treat them gingerly. It is permissible to hire one or two professors who know their fields, but let it be distinctly understood that they will have nothing to do with deciding policy. Anything that can be described as your "brain trust" is to be shunned with all the devices of concealment and dissembling your staff can dream up.

This taboo does not apply to movie stars, ball players, actors, television comedians, female radio philosophers and other celebrities. Comes an election year and these types yearn to get into the act. Since roughly 50 per cent of them will be on your side, by the law of averages, you may as well take advantage of them. There is no reliable evidence that a man who tells jokes on TV, or who bats .352 in the National League, is necessarily a canny judge of Presidential candidates, but the legend thrives that he is. You may pick up a scattering of votes from those who find you personally unimpressive but will take a night-club comic's word that you are something special. Anyway, no political show ever suffered from the appearance of a Hollywood cutie.

As you broaden your acquaintances among men in your own party, you'll find they range from responsible, intelligent chaps down to those who should be in a psychiatric ward, if not in jail. Some of the latter are bound to express opinions you can't possibly endorse. Your cue here is to toss off some glib pontification about your party being big enough to embrace many points of view and "of course" you don't have to agree with everyone on every issue. (You couldn't; politics is flexible but not *that* flexible.) You can also explain that your differences are only of degree. This will be true, in the sense that the difference between drought and flood is one of degree.

Groups deserving your closest attention are the political hacks of your own party who will infest your campaign train. From them, according to a harmless fancy, you will get common sense, practical advice and "realistic reports" on what the people are thinking. For them, according to another equally innocent notion, your mere presence provides just the push their local campaign needs.

Most of the other candidates in your party—the would-be governors, congressmen, aldermen, sheriffs and so on—will be total strangers to you. Hail them warmly and get their names straight when you tell your audience how happy you are to be on the same ticket with "my good friend, Timothy J. Schlump." Others will be all too well known to you, to your regret. If you are elected, you can expect from them the same co-operation the Hatfields used to get from the McCoys. Forget all this. Put in a plug for them and hope they'll show their appreciation. It's possible they may— until the election is over.

At informal meetings with machine politicians you may become downright chummy. Boast that you are a "politician and proud of it." Such remarks are kept off the record; the general public might not understand. Let yourself go a little at these affairs. Denounce the smug, self-righteous citizen who imagines himself too good for the rough and tumble of politics. Praise the ward heeler and his doorbell ringers as the backbone of working democracy. Your audience will lap this up. Politics has its rewards, but a kind word is seldom among them.

In return for the compliments, your listeners will bring you "encouraging reports." This is a fact; the politician hasn't been born who won't issue an encouraging report. On the basis of these, plus your own "independent surveys," you detect trends and groundswells, all portending a landslide victory.

It is sometimes safe to pick out a politician in your own party who has managed to infuriate a sizable bloc of voters, and announce courageously that you will not support him. Try to select one who is not up for re-election at the time. He is less likely to take offense. At any rate, denouncing someone in *your* party stamps you as a man of lofty principle. Unless your target is convinced you mean it, you can make your peace with him after the election and he will understand.

Like all professionals, politicians love to talk shop. Away from the office most of them—even those of the opposition— are a deceptively likeable lot. There must, however, be no fraternizing with the enemy. Treatment of the opposition, in fact, is a special phase of campaigning, which may now be considered briefly.

15

The Rascals, In or Out

"I don't propose to enter into any debate."
—WILLIAM P. VILAS, Wisconsin

THE CANDIDATE nominated by the other party may be more glamorous, more popular, handsomer, a better talker, wealthier and (anything is possible) smarter than you. For your purposes, this is all beside the point. Publicly, express deep satisfaction that he has been chosen to run against you. This will make the issues "crystal clear," you say, so that the people will be able to see the vast, fundamental differences between the two parties. (Don't try to spell them out.)

From there, indicate that you are most anxious to have the campaign conducted on issues, not personalities. When you are asked about your opponent, respond in vaguely indulgent terms as if he were a misguided child. Generally you don't mention your opponent by name at all. The technique is to behave as if you are running against a nameless ghost. You had better observe this ancient custom even though it makes little sense. (Professional politicians have an explanation for it; they say it cuts down the opponent's publicity: Frankly, though, you won't be able to keep his name out of the papers or off the air.)

Even the shrewdest campaigner makes mistakes and your opposite number may stumble into saying something grossly unpopular. In this event (first making sure he *has* put his foot in it) you get around the unmentionable name by observing "there are those who say" and then ripping into the boner in question.

At some point, quote a dead hero of the opposition party, declare that you agree wholeheartedly with his sentiments and demand accusingly whether your adversary can say the same. Stealing the greats of the other party is a tactic deeply imbedded in our traditions. It has little effect on the voters, but it must be done. Besides, even the most partisan saint of the opposition party has said something broad and general you can underwrite. Don't attempt any dangerous innovations in making this play. Democrats should quote Lincoln at the enemy; Republicans should stick with Jefferson.

You might tie this in with another hallowed campaign maneuver when you challenge your opponent to a public debate. Throw down the gage (observing the no-name rule) to the "other candidate" and insist that he meet you "on the same platform" to thresh out the issues. Mention the Lincoln-

Douglas debates, which have a nostalgic appeal in no way diminished by the fact that Lincoln and Douglas were not contesting for the Presidency at the time.

You will be pretty safe in thus daring your opponent. Since there is no reason why he should let you run *his* campaign he will almost certainly decline. When he does, your staff of interpreters can scoff that he is afraid. If he beats you to the draw with a challenge of his own, observe loftily that such a debate "would serve no useful purpose." Add that you see no reason why you should lend the use of your name to give him free publicity.

Voters in impressive numbers will be whooping it up for your antagonist; brush them off as "machine politicians." Any of his campaign tactics, especially one that seems to be getting results, is "a shameless display of politics for which the people will show their resentment at the polls." Politics, of course, is the very thing you're trying to get the voters interested in. Still, it's a dirty word.

The other party's platform, for your purposes, is always a "hodge-podge of glittering generalities" and its record is a "tragic history of muddling and bungling." If it happens to be in power, it will obviously try to "buy votes with public funds." If it is just trying to elbow its way into office, you may accuse it of a bare-faced attempt to sell out the government to predatory interests.

This sort of free-wheeling denunciation seems to generate its own momentum and you may be carried away to the point where you accuse your opponent flatly of being a crook. Reporters will be on to you before you can get your foot out of your mouth.

Do you *really* mean, they'll want to know, that the other candidate is a thief, that he's stolen something—ought to be in jail, perhaps?

It's up to you to weasel out as best you can. You were not questioning your adversary's personal honesty, you may concede; you were merely pointing out that his party's policies, if carried out, would rob the people of their birthright.

The weakness of this feeble elaboration cannot be disguised. Guard your tongue. To have to confess that your opponent should not be behind bars can be most embarrassing.

Whether you run as an "in" or an "out" the opposition will do something you can't condemn wholeheartedly. If you are "in," grab credit for anything the other side has forced you to do. If, even from the outside, you have to admit some opposition scheme is not wholly devoid of merit, you may announce that "of course" you would not abandon the fundamental principles of the thing. You would, however, put it on a sound basis, eliminating "red tape" and "needless expenditures."

Your competitor, or the brains behind him, may be just tricky enough, or lucky enough, to go prospecting for a fool-proof promise and strike pay dirt. It is best to be prepared for unfair competition of this sort. Suppose he has sketched out his idea only in broad outline. Challenge him to tell how it would work—in other words to be specific. (This, remember, is the very thing you've been trying to dodge.) If, on the other hand, he has perfected all the details, you may approve the "broad features" of his plan but protest that the ways and means should be left up to Congress and should not be imposed by a dictator.

To cover all possibilities, let's imagine the worst. Your rival, or his party, has hit upon a scheme which the public hails with unanimous acclaim. Your position is almost desperate but not quite. Point out blandly that, chiefly through the generosity of *your* party, "general agreement" has been reached on this issue and it has now been taken out of politics. Then drop the whole thing. This countermove is, admittedly, a makeshift, but politics is like warfare: you must do the best you can with what you have.

One probable development should be mentioned, not because it is important in itself but to guard you against surprise. At some point in the campaign you can count on an announcement that a national committee of members of the opposite party has been organized to support *you*. This may give you a warm glow, but don't kid yourself. There is no revolution afoot. At best, it means that a disgruntled politician has been cold-shouldered by your opponent and is just showing his spite. He won't bring you many votes.

The same thing holds true when a national committee of members of *your* party comes out for the election of your foe. This is why we caution you; don't be stung into a hasty remark about rats leaving the sinking ship. From your point of view this would hardly be the *mot juste*.

Be prepared, too, to suffer petty annoyances at the hands of lesser figures in the enemy camp. You'll be threatened with arrest because your motor parade zoomed through some town you never heard of. This means nothing, except that the mayor of the town is against you and has his own campaign worries.

The opposition will be spreading rumors about you and you'll hear about them. You'll be asked to comment on reports that you left college owing a tailor bill or that you

132

have an ugly criminal record of passing a red light 20 years ago. Dismiss these airily with "They must be pretty desperate, spreading nonsense like that." And pay the tailor.

One final word: Sometimes, through carelessness or mismanagement on the part of one or both of the campaign chairmen, your path may cross your opponent's and the two of you will meet face to face. This is like unsound currency —it is to be avoided at all hazards. If it should occur, there is nothing for either of you to do but behave like grown men and greet each other pleasantly. Such conduct has no place in a political campaign.

16

A Few Simple Rules

". . . always clear, concise and intelligent . . ."
—J. R. WILLIAMS, Illinois

THERE IS a tendency on the part of political novices—a perfectly natural one—to conceive of the ideal campaign speech as a clear, interesting and orderly marshaling of irrefutable arguments on one side of a controversial issue. The error would be laughable if its consequences were not so serious. Your laudable impulse to speak out boldly on any debatable proposition must be stifled mercilessly. It gets down to this: Why rile the hornets unnecessarily?

The campaign speech is not an end; it is a means. It is the excuse for putting on the main show, the means of getting your face and voice on nation-wide hookups, the plausible reason for beating about the country like a medicine man, which, in effect, you are. A speaking tour, thoughtfully scheduled and shrewdly promoted, can provide endless opportunities for you to run through your bag of tricks, to show yourself in numerous roles: thinker, worrier about the fate of the nation, robust he-man. Speeches are important in the same way that mortar is important to bricks.

You write your own speeches (of course). As Willkie put it, "I roll my own." This is to persuade people that you are a born phrase-maker, perhaps another Lincoln in that line, assured of a good half column in Bartlett's quotations.

Surprisingly, many people will assume that you *do* write your own and their belief will persist even when, before their very eyes, you elbow your way through a squad of ghost writers to get to the mike.

At the microphone you'll encounter one of the peculiarities of campaign speechmaking. Years ago your college debating coach may have advised you to stand quietly, surveying your audience with easy confidence before you begin to talk. Forget that. As you step forward, the crowd, with local ward heelers egging it on, is stamping and cheering tumultuously, stripped of all reason by the previous speaker's stunning disclosure that he was introducing "the next President of the United States." Dignified reserve on your part would be out of place. Raise your arms above your head and wave them jubilantly, like a punch-drunk but victorious prize fighter. This helps convince the audience that you share their enthusiasm and are not too high and mighty to show it.

You must let it be known at the outset of your campaign that you will (of course) deal only in facts. People expect this, although there is no record of any candidate starting out by announcing that he would appeal only to passion and prejudice. Early in the campaign it makes the voters feel virtuous to reflect that everything *their* candidate will say will be the exact, literal truth about a given issue. Tell them you're their man.

If you are an able speaker—that is, better than your opponent—you have an advantage you may legitimately ex-

ploit for all it's worth. You'd better get an objective opinion on this point. Any self-delusion about it is bound to boomerang. A voice that sounds sonorous in the bathroom can be pretty reedy on the rear platform of a campaign train.

The chances are you're not too good. It is one of the penalties you must pay now for the years of silence when you were minding your own business and letting other people mind theirs. You may take refuge in the explanation, offered by friends, that you are no spellbinder and don't pretend to be. All you ask is the chance to discuss the issues in language anybody can understand, without tricks or flourishes. Such devices as clear, coherent sentences or neatly turned phrases, you imply, are meant only to deceive the voter, something you wouldn't dream of doing.

This is all very well. Still, the way you speak will draw attention and comment. Hire a speech expert to make you sound at least intelligible. For a small extra fee he should be able to analyze your accent with some very interesting results. It is, he'll find, typically American with traces, say, of New England twang (without the nasal quality), a Southern drawl (but a little sharper) and Midwestern flatness (ever so slightly rounded). The report of this dissection of your speech should be made public, to help the voters make up their minds.

The mere fact that you are committed to writing your own addresses need not prevent you from seeking "the best advice." Proclaim this openly. You are sensible enough to realize that one man can't know the details of every subject. Invite assorted experts to go over these "complex, vital problems" with you. Elder statesmen of your party will accept these invitations gratefully; your problem may be in keeping them away.

The experts will serve cheerfully without pay, other than the unaccustomed and heady publicity they receive. What's more, they can be reminded to leave a consultation with you shaking their heads in awe at your amazing grasp of intricate fields of knowledge to which they have devoted their entire lives. They highlight details of the picture of you as an openminded patriot who listens to all sides, then makes up his own mind. You welcome advice, you say, but the final decision on what goes into your speeches is made by you alone.

You will engage in no smears. This happens to be true but say it anyway. Smears and mud-slinging may be entrusted confidently to other members of your team. Furthermore, you will conduct your campaign in "the white light of merciless publicity." For one thing, there's no other place *to* conduct it. Nevertheless, the statement has a useful connotation —that your opponent will sneak furtively around the country on *his* campaign, letting no one know what sinister things he is up to.

With these general observations out of the way, we may get down to the fine points of political oratory. It is beyond the scope of the present work to furnish complete texts. Your ghost writers will have to "write your own," but they may avoid disastrous blunders if they observe a few elementary rules.

The first is this: Don't be a hero. You are not trying to win votes with speeches; you are trying not to lose them. There is no point in lashing out at something that large segments of the population may like. Save the heroics for denouncing causes supported only by criminals and idiots. Otherwise, be careful, mighty careful.

"But," you will object, "this leaves me nothing to talk about." This is a common error, traceable to your essential, precandidacy good sense. It is nothing to be alarmed about. The field for riskless denunciation is bounded only by the human imagination. You can shoot the works against corruption, hammer unidentified special interests until they reel. The most shameless crooks and grafters will assume that you are talking about someone else when you assail corruption. Nobody ever considered himself a special interest. You can lambaste waste, extravagance and penny-pinching, incompetence, inefficiency, selfishness and greed, those who would turn the clock back and dangerous experimenters. All of these targets are safe and will suggest many more.

Second is the rule of But and However. If this rule did not exist, it would be necessary to invent it. It helps you skim over thin ice with complete confidence. It works this way: You are in favor of something *but* not enough to worry anybody who's against it. You are for helping Europe *but* not at the expense of Asia. We must guard our interests in Asia, always remembering, *however*, that we cannot ignore Europe. This technique is handy for snatching at an issue that has been grabbed by the opposition. It also helps slide around some unpopular thing your party may have done. You know taxes are necessary *but* you're by no means sold on the present rates. This program has been enacted; you realize, *however*, that it may not be perfect. It's like throwing a punch and keeping your guard up.

Third is the Rule of the Greased Word. It calls for the judicious selection of words that sound authoritative, look impressive in print and pin you down to nothing. Here are a few examples: You will "promote" education. You will "foster" the development of electric-power programs. You will "protect" the rights of labor and management. You are for "long-range plans" to do this and for the "eventual" accomplishment of that. There are hundreds of words in this category and they must be chosen with nice discrimination.

You may demand a "more realistic level" of tips to waiters and everyone will love you. The careless use of "lower level" would infuriate the waiters and "high level" would antagonize the customers. Likewise, promise to "promote good will in labor relations" and both sides will beam happily. Get more specific and one side or the other is going to be voting for your opponent.

Fourth is the Rule of Unswerving Devotion. It covers the concepts to which all candidates cling, but it cannot, simply for that reason, be taken for granted. Omissions will be pounced on by the opposition as evidence of your unfitness.

Tradition requires that you speak out, keeping your guard high as indicated in Rule Two. As we noted in an earlier chapter, you insist on a sound currency at "all hazards." You are for a stronger, better America. You demand impregnable defenses, consistent, of course, with our ability to pay for them. You favor a strong international organization for peace based, naturally, on principles of law and justice to which all nations will subscribe. You advocate a balanced budget. Possibly, in view of your party's record, this bare statement might draw mocking laughs. In that case you may promise to "work toward" a balanced budget. You are for making "full use" of our natural resources, but don't destroy the clean simplicity of this statement with gingerbready details.

Finally, these words and phrases must be strung together with another set of expressions tested by experience. You don't simply believe; you are "firmly of the opinion." It is not enough merely to oppose; you are an "uncompromising foe of" or "unalterably opposed to." You are "dedicated to the proposition that," "stand four square" and have "unshakable faith in." Your campaign, once more, is a "crusade" to restore to the people the sort of government that is their "rightful heritage." The temptation to improve on these phrases or to substitute your own will be almost irresistible. Don't weaken. They have stood the test of time; they are slogans that sell. Novelties like "two cars in every garage" or "horse-and-buggy days" have been known to backlash.

17

The Varnished Truth

"We are looking into the promised land."
—J. FRANKLIN FORT, New Jersey

WITH THESE guides memorized—a re-reading after the convention would not be wasted—you are ready to take off. You made an opening speech when you first decided to go after the nomination, remember? You made another when you accepted it. Now you are poised for still more openings.

A single "opening speech of the campaign" would impose a needless handicap on the candidate. Possibly his timing would be off; the weather might be too hot, the voters on vacation and simply not interested. It takes time for a candidate and his ghost writers to learn to work together. One of their first productions could easily fall flat and leave the electorate apathetic.

There's an easy way around this. Your campaign staff can bill an early address as the "informal" opening of your drive. If it comes off, well and good. But you may need a "preview" opening in some other part of the country or an "official" opening in still another. Just keep at it until you strike the happy combination—a passable speech, perfect weather and a holiday atmosphere that seems to spark noticeable enthusiasm. This, your staff may confide to reporters, was the "real" kickoff to your campaign.

After that, you get down to specific generalities in a series of speeches that follows a pattern as precise as the stately measures of a minuet. There's the farm speech, delivered before an audience in galluses and overalls; the labor speech before a union convention; the foreign-policy speech; the national-defense speech; and so on. Skip any one of these and your opponent will proclaim happily that you are "afraid to speak out" on this topic or that.

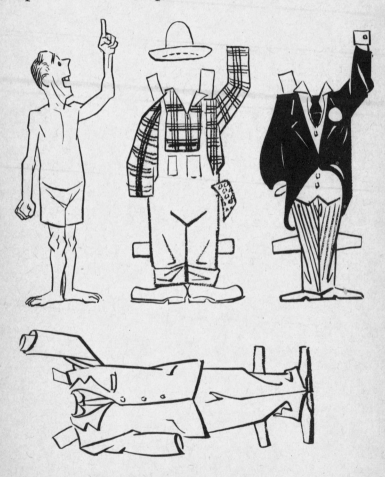

There's no need to run this risk. Even if you are convinced you have nothing particularly original or significant to contribute on some issue, the approach is easy to master. Suppose your party is out of office. Start by tracing the miserable, intolerable conditions which are making so many people unhappy today. (The best-heeled, best-fed of your supporters will nod agreement with this uncannily accurate description of their plight.) Then, after a few more references to the "misrule" which brought all this on, glide swiftly over your own proposals for a change—something like "We, the American people, can do better than this." Get into a glowing account of the glorious days that lie ahead—with what by now should be called your "infectious smile"—when you have dealt with, say, the cost-of-living problem. Some slight adjustments must be made if your party happens to be in power. In this case, your opening passage should be a harrowing description of how terrible things were before *that* happy event. Pick it up from there, concluding on a note of confidence that, under experienced guidance, things will keep on getting better.

One speech requires special care. Campaign managers cherish many notions based on assumptions ranging from the debatable to the ludicrous. One of these is the belief that there is a "women's vote," that it is decisive (especially in *this* election) and that it can be sewed up by the candidate who appears before gatherings arranged by lady politicians. No doubt at least one such appearance will be set up for you. (This is one place where an unmarried candidate has a decided advantage over his more domesticated rival.)

This is your chance to extend yourself. Your clumsiest compliments, your most outrageous flattery will draw appreciative giggles. Go to the other extreme of deadpan gravity in attributing to women every conceivable political virtue—thrift, honesty, common sense and a fierce desire to protect our children and our children's children. Promise to give women their "rightful" representation in your administration. (This will terrify some men, but your staff can give

private assurances that you have no intention, for instance, of appointing a woman Secretary of Defense. They might even intimate that the most ardent antifeminist will be more than pleased when he learns what you mean by "rightful.") Say that if only women controlled the government it would be bursting with integrity and efficiency, free of graft, misjudgment, waste and all other ills. This may strike you as fanciful, even preposterous, but don't hold back. The women expect it. Men will understand.

Since many of these speeches will be broadcast by radio and television, they present a problem in tactics which cannot be ignored. At every meeting the platform will be jammed with the inevitable hangers-on—local candidates, contributors, the more influential bosses and the like. Several of these will precede you as speakers. You can't prevent it. They help to get the show going, but the lure of a nation-wide audience will be too much for some of them. *They* will keep on speaking on the time *you* are paying for, and paying plenty. You must be firm to the point of ruthlessness about this. It is no time for false modesty about your appeal as a speaker and much less for politeness. Don't use force if you can avoid it, but make sure that you, and not the local candidate for coroner, have the mike when the time comes to go on the air.

Every candidate, including the most cautious, will at times slip a line into a speech which he later regrets. Fatigue plays funny tricks and applause may goad one into recklessness. Regardless of why, the candidate may relax for a moment and become specific. The animals—some in your own party, all in the opposition—will set up a howl. If this happens to you it is up to your staff to get you off the hook. One or two friends, perhaps a visiting congressman or senator from your party—may be detailed to give out a special interpretation of the offending statement which makes it perfectly clear that what you really meant was substantially different from what you actually said. Even if the difference is startling, don't worry about it.

Any boner in that line can easily be offset by another bit of stage business. You stroll up to the lectern, speech in hand, ready to give voice to another of your ghost writers' effusions. Wait until the racket subsides and you have everybody's attention. Then tear up the speech impulsively and announce that you're going to "talk from the heart."

This is foolproof if you keep a carbon copy of the speech handy to bolster your memory as you rattle on "from the heart." It creates a warm impression of independence and forthrightness more valuable than anything you could possibly say. The audience, forgetting that Lincoln did pretty well at Gettysburg with a prepared speech, will be convinced that tearing up that copy makes you one with the nation's heroes.

The Last Speech of the campaign is in a special category and can spark more arguments than the T-formation vs. the Single Wing. One school favors a fighting finish, one last shotgun blast at the opposition. The other insists on the Calm Appeal.

Frankly, we lean toward the Calm Appeal. The time is Election Eve, the occasion a nation-wide broadcast. For once you won't have to battle for your time through hordes of local politicians. This one can be staged in a studio, the set a book-lined office. You urge your listeners to cast aside any bitterness and then you make the calm appeal to all citizens to get out and vote. You don't care how they vote (you say) just so they vote. It's not so much what you say; it's the way you say it. A good Calm Appeal can create a very convincing air of confidence, while the Shotgun is apt to sound panicky. Still, the Shotgun may have a bracing effect on some voters. The question of which is best cannot be answered dogmatically.

18

Lincoln's Law

YOU HAVE MADE your Last Speech; you have waged your campaign. You have run for President. There's nothing much more you can do except go home and try to sleep it off.

The sudden shift in your role, from active to passive, may be a shock. The whirlwind you helped to sow has spent its force, but its dying gusts will sweep you along a little longer. There are a few odd jobs still to be done, and you will find yourself going through the motions automatically.

On Election Day you vote early in company with your wife, if you have one. You exude confidence as you do so. Regardless of the weather—sunny, stormy or in between—you profess to see in it a favorable omen. You smile and one last picture of the amiable candidate makes the television screens and the newspapers.

Election night you may go to your campaign headquarters or stay at home; it doesn't make much difference. It's too late to swing any votes, but you still express optimism. Don't make any predictions, however. The payoff is too close for that.

Draft two telegrams. One is the wire you hope you'll never send. It conveys your congratulations to your victorious opponent and pledges him your support. Don't overdo it. Your side has been portraying him too plainly as an incompetent, spineless, wrong-thinking muddler to allow for a complete about-face on such short notice.

The other is the telegram you hope to dispatch. It thanks your rival for sending *his* telegram of congratulations. No gloating in this, but don't let your gratitude sound too lavish, either. He probably meant some of the things he said about you.

If you send the victor's telegram, you are on your own so far as this work is concerned. Should you send the loser's you will, understandably, be disappointed. Political post-mortems are of doubtful value, but they always follow elections and sometimes drag on for years. Looking back, you'll see where you made mistakes. Don't berate yourself too harshly for them. Just possibly you may have overlooked a basic rule to which allusion has been made.

Remember Lincoln's Law: You can't fool all of the people all of the time.

About the Authors

CHARLES ELLIS *is an editorial writer for the Philadelphia* Inquirer. *He has been observing politics and politicians since he graduated from Princeton University with, appropriately, a degree in politics.*

He has been a police reporter and a City Hall reporter, was the Washington correspondent for the Inquirer *before and after the war, and covered the 1940 campaign with Franklin D. Roosevelt (who, Mr. Ellis says, needed no books like this one to tell him how to do it).*

Mr. Ellis was a personnel officer in the Navy during the war. His brief experience as a political publicist in Washington taught him that (a) he liked most politicians and (b) he wasn't one. He is married and has three children.

FRANK WEIR *also is a reporter and writer for the Philadelphia* Inquirer. *He has covered the conventions and campaigns of each presidential election since Alf Landon popularized the Sunflower in Cleveland. With one exception. A previous engagement with the U.S. Navy prevented him from attending the political exercises of 1944.*

A Philadelphian, Mr. Weir has been a newspaperman since shortly after his graduation from Penn State. About half his experience has been as a correspondent in Washington. He himself has two of the leading qualifications for a candidate—a wife and a young daughter.